The Comic Book Guide to the Mission

A Cartoon Tour Through San Francisco's Mission District

Collected and Edited by Lauren Davis
Skoda Man Press

The Comic Book Guide to the Mission:
A Cartoon Tour Through San Francisco's Mission District
Published by Skoda Man Press

Compilation copyright © 2010 Skoda Man Press.
All content copyright © 2009-2010 by respective creators unless otherwise noted.

All rights reserved.

All characters herein and distinctive likenesses thereof are properties of the respective creators. No portion of this book may be reprinted or reproduced (except for review purposes) without written permission from the creators.

ISBN: 978-0-9831103-0-9

www.skodaman.com

Concept/Editor: Lauren Davis
Cover Illustration: Chuck Whelon

Printed in Canada.

Table of Contents

Fragments in the Mission..1
By Jamaica Dyer

Adobe Bookshop..4
By Aindrila Mukhopadhyay

Murray the Attorney..5
Story by Clint Woods, Art by Nomi Kane

Nothing About Nothing..10
By Rick Worley

Weird Fish..14
By Aindrila Mukhopadhyay

Buy Used, Buy Bulk..15
By Alfred Twu

Down on Mission Street..20
By Geoff Vasile

Roxie..25
By Aindrila Mukhopadhyay

Luna Park..26
By Aindrila Mukhopadhyay

The Mission Taco..27
Story by Omar Mamoon, Art by Greg Hinkle

Beretta..36
By Aindrila Mukhopadhyay

Veintidós..37
By Dan V.

Fourteenth & Mission..42
By Sean Chiki

Fair Weather Friends..45
By Amy Martin

O Valencia! 46
By Andrew Farago and Shaenon K. Garrity

Jason. 48
By Roman Muradov

Consuming. 49
By Roman Muradov

No one will ever love me anymore. 50
By Roman Muradov

How to screw up Craigslist interviews. 51
By Roman Muradov

Hip. 52
By Roman Muradov

Mission Statements 53
By Mario Hernandez

A True Travel Tale 56
By Justin Hall

SF Dyke March 57
By Ariel Schrag

Field Notes from the Hipster Habitat 62
Story by Matt Stewart, Art by John Mathis

Boogaloo's 67
By Aindrila Mukhopadhyay

All Over Coffee #396 68
By Paul Madonna

What Hazel Eats 71
By Jonas Madden-Connor

Eight Blocks 72
By Jen Oaks

Amnesia...75
By Aindrila Mukhopadhyay

The Murals of the Mission...76
By Jeff Walker

Amity Blamity Presents: The Mission....................................81
By Mike White

Places Seen in the Comics..84

Contributor Bios..88

Acknowledgments & Notes...94

A COUPLE YEARS LATER...

I'm in college, and we'd pile into a car and drive to SF to crash our animation teacher's party at a swanky bar in the Mission.

A couple years after THAT I'm in the Mission celebrating my first job.

After a long day at work, I'd sit in the park with my friend and over cheap wine we'd have crazy introspective conversations about where life is going.

SOON...

I go on this first date with my new boyfriend.

We go on this epic bar crawl...

and I'm so distracted by him, that I have no idea where I am.

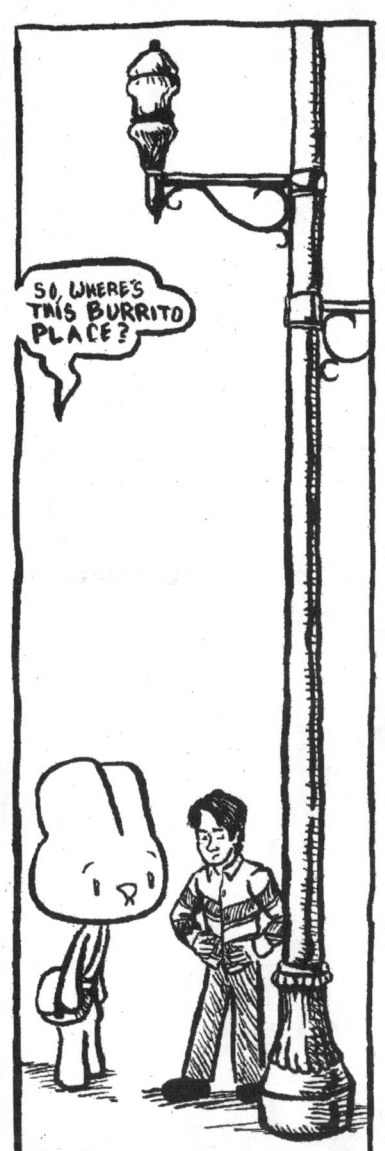

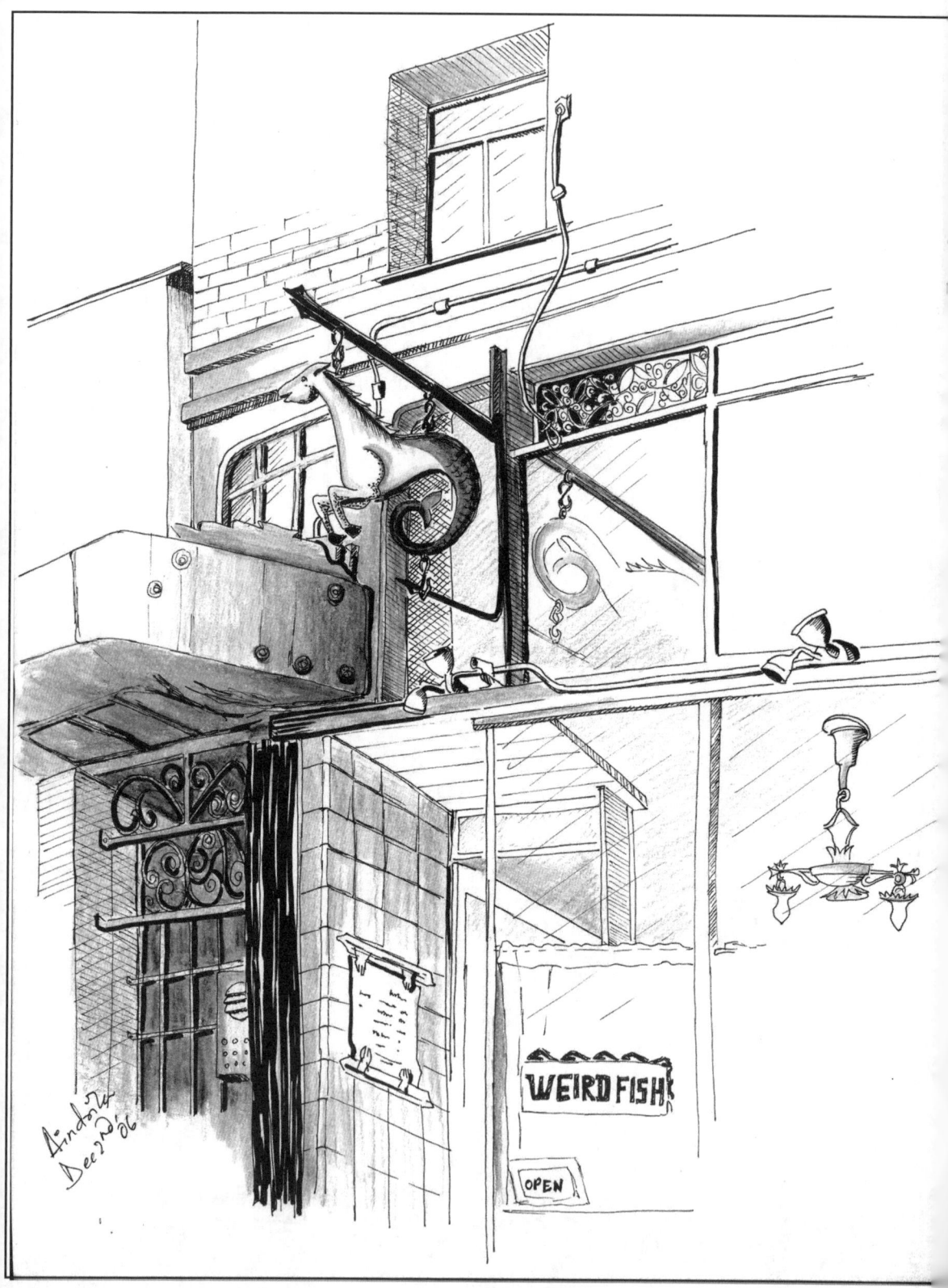

The layout of every thrift store is a lot like a typical department store: random small things in the front, clothing left and right, furniture, housewares, and books in the back — wait a minute, department stores don't sell books! What does that say about our society?

Anyway, on to today's first item: bowls!

If you've got a friend visiting from out of town looking for a souvenir, show them the miscellany aisles of your favorite thrift store!

In addition to T-shirts and knickknacks, I've come across mix tapes and even the occasional home video!

I used to think we used plates more often than bowls as we had far more plates in the pantry. But one day it was pointed out that bowls are used more, which is why there aren't as many left in the pantry! So now I just get bowls. Small bowls. They encourage folks to take less food at a time, reducing food waste. Since bowls keep getting broken I've also been getting stainless steel ones. There's been a little grumbling about the prison look, though not as much as that one time I brought home doggie dishes.

I keep having to buy new silverware as well. This one's a little harder to explain at first but I found my answer while auditing the trash one day. Lazy hippies!

NOT CHEAP ENOUGH?
Community Thrift has half price sales every month on the first Monday (everything) and the third Monday (clothing only)

And done! Next stop... Blank clothing for screenprinting!

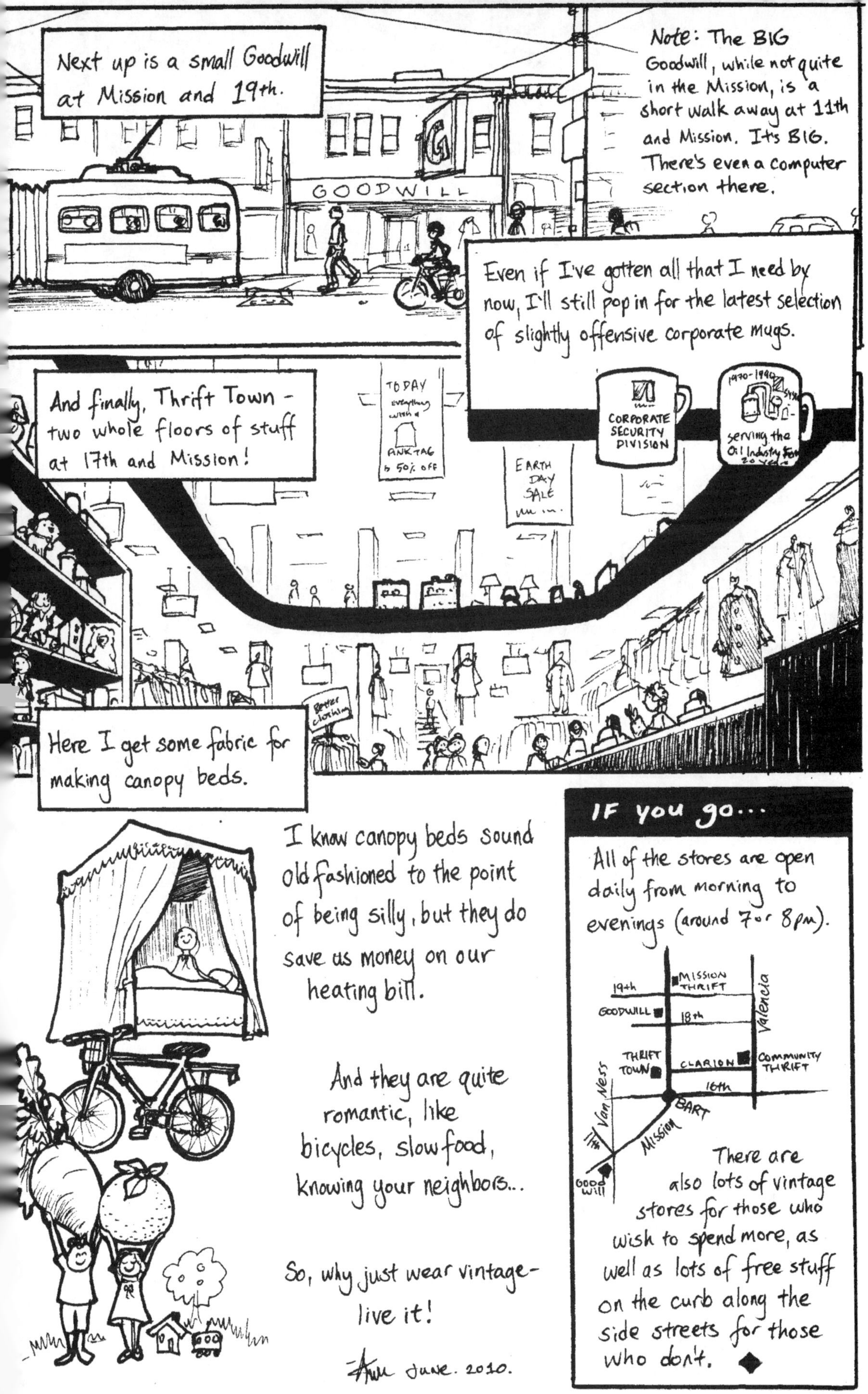

Next up is a small Goodwill at Mission and 19th.

Note: The BIG Goodwill, while not quite in the Mission, is a short walk away at 11th and Mission. It's BIG. There's even a computer section there.

Even if I've gotten all that I need by now, I'll still pop in for the latest selection of slightly offensive corporate mugs.

And finally, Thrift Town — two whole floors of stuff at 17th and Mission!

Here I get some fabric for making canopy beds.

I know canopy beds sound old fashioned to the point of being silly, but they do save us money on our heating bill.

And they are quite romantic, like bicycles, slow food, knowing your neighbors...

So, why just wear vintage — live it!

— Aku June 2010.

IF you go...

All of the stores are open daily from morning to evenings (around 7 or 8 pm).

There are also lots of vintage stores for those who wish to spend more, as well as lots of free stuff on the curb along the side streets for those who don't. ◆

TAQUERIA VALLARTA

AFTER A LONG DAY OF MOVING ALL MY STUFF INTO MY NEW APARTMENT, I WANDERED AROUND 24TH ST. FOR A LITTLE BIT, HOPING TO POP MY MISSION TACO CHERRY. ALL I HAD TO DO WAS FOLLOW MY NOSE.

THEY'RE SMART FOLKS OVER AT VALLARTA, LET ME TELL YOU. THEY POST A TRADITIONAL TACO GRILL STATION RIGHT NEAR THE FRONT DOOR. THIS CLEVER SETUP PRODUCES A HEAVENLY AROMA THAT CAN BE SMELLED A MILE AWAY.

FIVE CARNE ASADA TACOS, PLEASE.

FIRST OFF, THE MEAT IS QUALITY. ALONG WITH GREAT QUALITY COMES GREAT FLAVOR, AND VALLARTA FILLS THEIR CARNE ASADA WITH TONS OF IT. THE MARINADE COUPLED WITH THE GREASE BATH CREATES A HEAVENLY TASTE. YOU COULD ALMOST EAT THE TACO SANS SALSA ROJA. BUT I WOULDN'T RECOMMEND IT, FOR THE SALSA ROJA HERE IS UNREAL.

BUT THE TACO HERE IS NOT PERFECT. THE MEAT TENDS TO BE DRIPPY AND OVERLY GREASY. THIS, COMBINED WITH THE SLIGHTLY UNDERCOOKED TORTILLAS RESULTED IN THE TACO BREAKING HALFWAY THROUGH THE MEAL. THIS IS A REAL SHAME, AS THE TORTILLA IS SIMULTANEOUSLY THE EASIEST THING TO EFF UP, AND THE EASIEST THING TO FIX.

WITH JUST A FEW TWEAKS TAQUERIA VALLARTA COULD'VE BEEN THE PERFECT TACO, AND FOR MY FIRST SOIREE IN THE MISH, IT WASN'T A BAD ONE.

Que Bueno.

AFTER WHAT SEEMED LIKE HOURS, OUR FOOD FINALLY ARRIVED. I'M JUST GOING TO BE BLUNT: IT WAS SHIT.

THE MEAT AND TORTILLAS WERE BURNT, AND THE SALSA ROJA WAS RUNNY AND TRANSPARENT. USUALLY WHEN I'M DRUNK I'LL EAT ANYTHING. BUT EVEN IN THIS STATE OF MIND, I REFUSED TO EAT MY SECOND TACO.

I'M NOT SURE IF KARMA HAD A ROLE IN THIS OR NOT, BUT UNFORTUNATELY FOR FAROLITO, I'M THE TACO GURU, SO I'LL HAVE THE LAST SAY. DO NOT EAT THE TACOS AT EL FAROLITO. THEY ARE

NO BUENO

"YOU GONNA EAT THAT?"

ON MY WAY OUT, I DID TAKE A BITE OF A HALF-EATEN QUESADILLA SUIZA (IT MAY HAVE BEEN POLLO ASADO) THAT SOMEONE LEFT BEHIND. THAT WAS ACTUALLY PRETTY DAMN GOOD.

Veintidós

Dan V. 2010

22ND ST

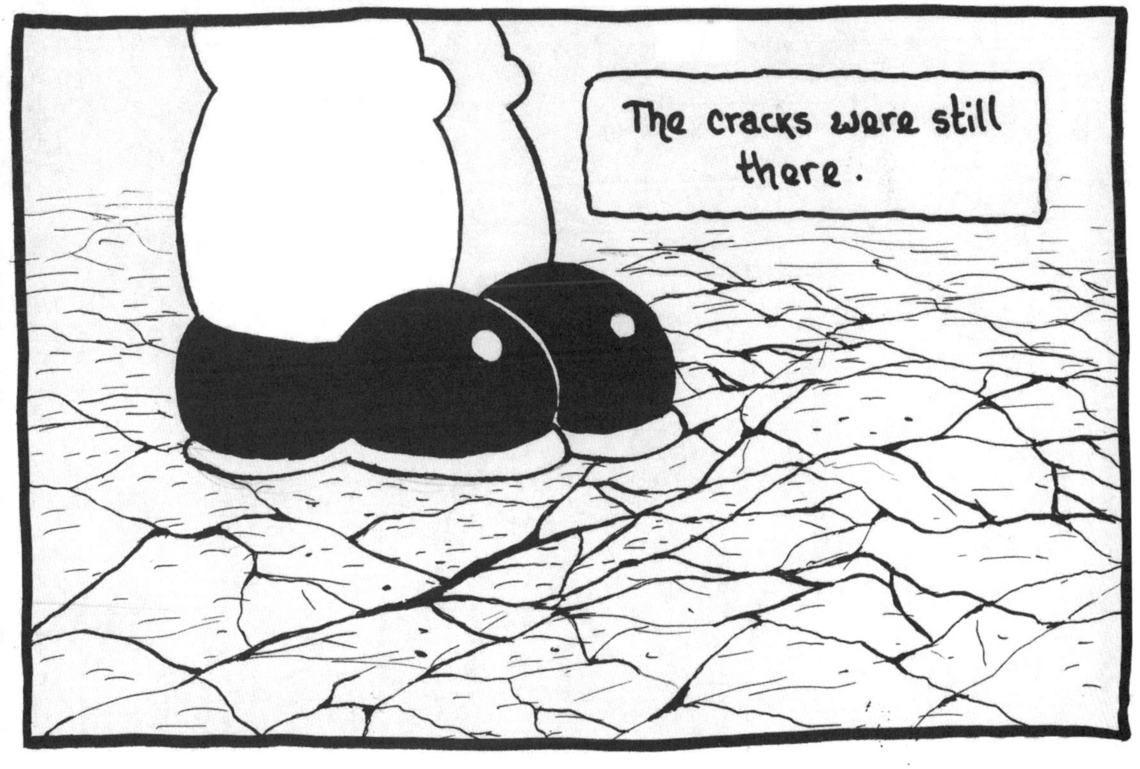

The cracks were still there.

As a child I remember staring at them, hoping for them to open wide enough for my tiny body to fit through. I had convinced myself that a different world existed underneath that very pavement. A world filled with miles of breathtaking landscapes and magical creatures. So I waited, night and day for the ground to open up.

It never did.

I had come to a conclusion that some of the inhabitants of the underworld were amongst us. Taking one look around 22nd and Mission, how could you doubt it?

It was filled with creatures that lurked in the shadows. They moaned at all hours of the night and in some instances, had epic battles in the middle of the streets!

Everyone in my neighborhood hated them. But not me, I had nothing but sympathy and compassion for the creatures. For I alone knew the sole reason for all their sadness...

22 years before...

I know why you're sad.

But dont worry Mr., the ground will open up soon.

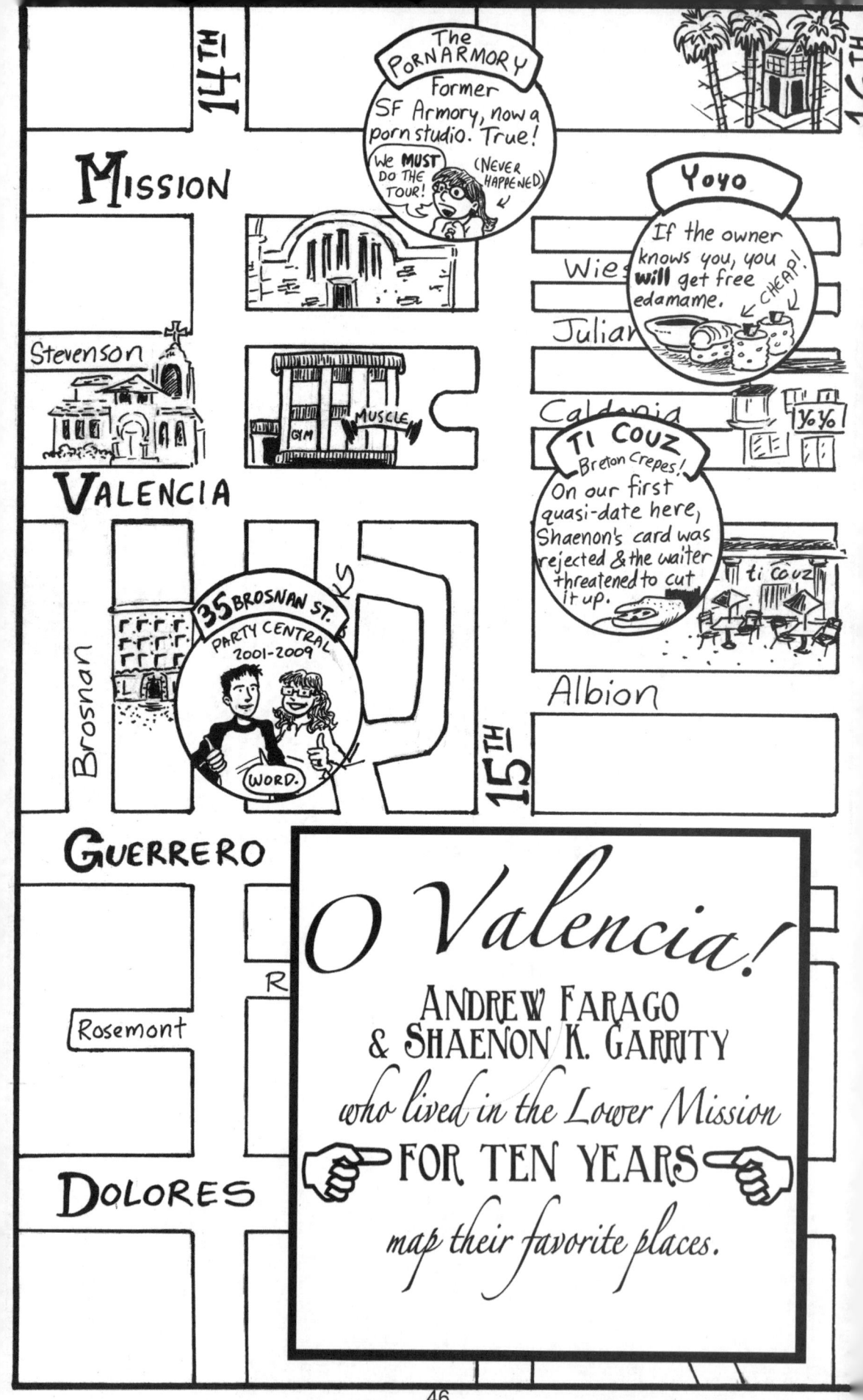

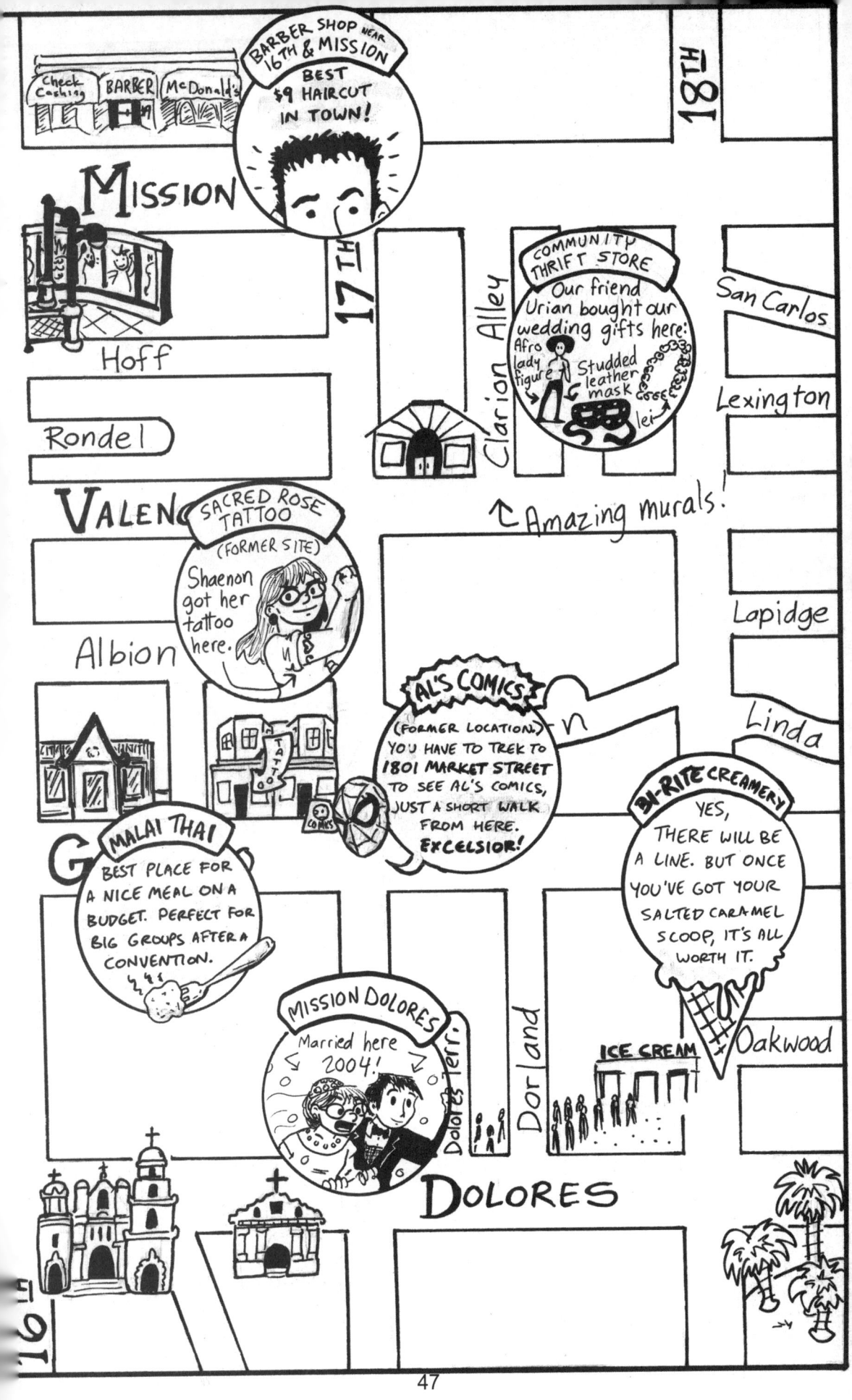

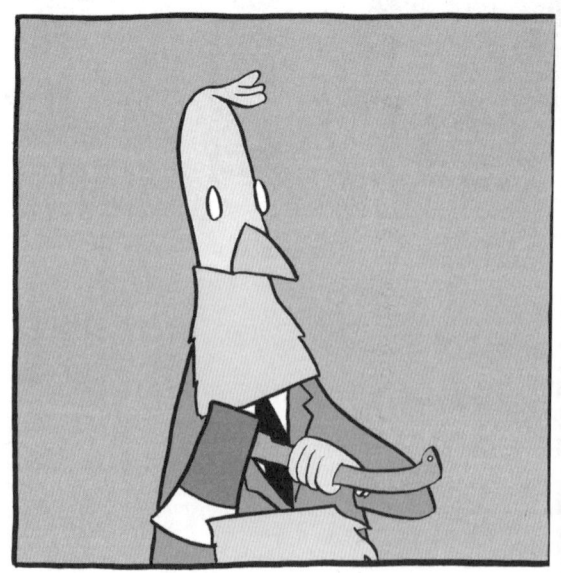

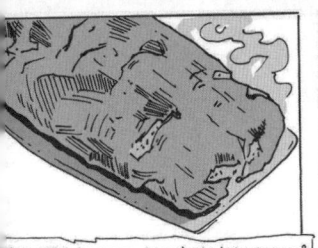

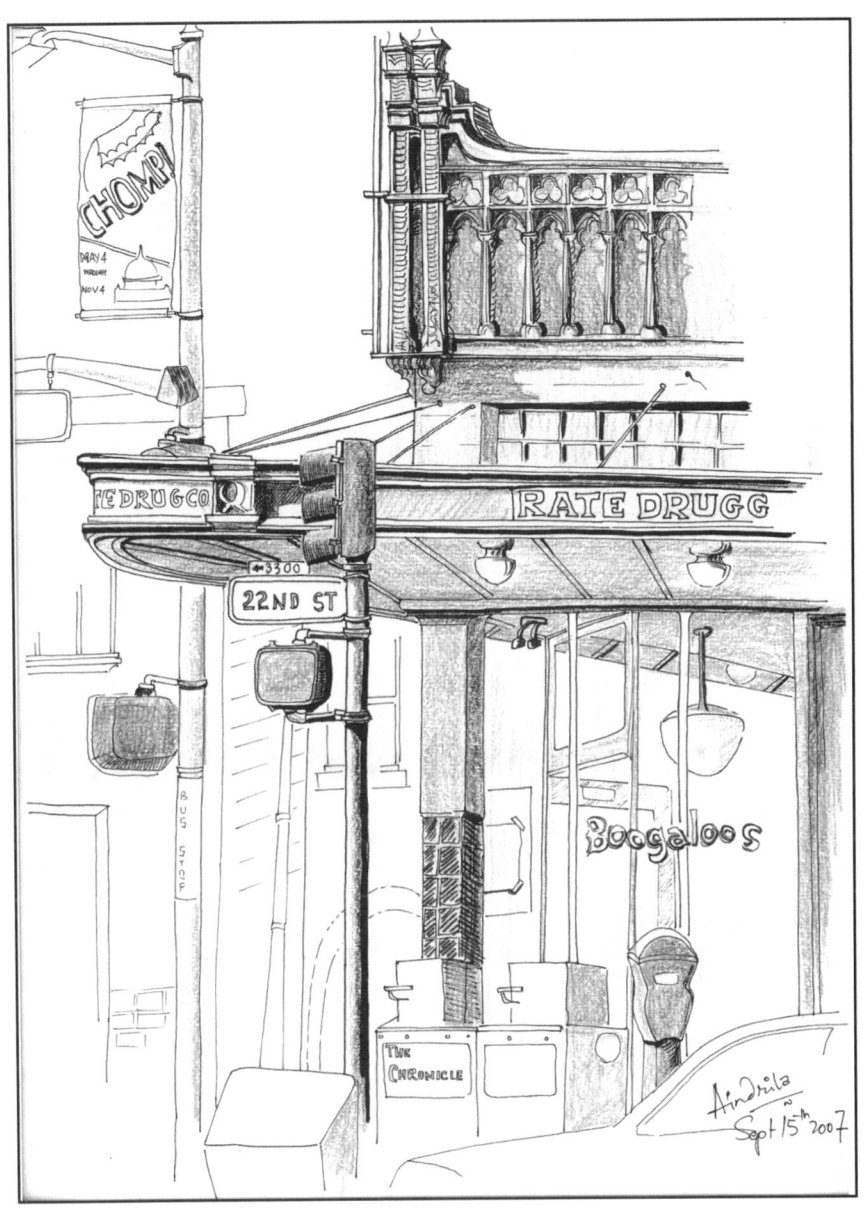

All the places we went,

things we did.

At one point I tried to arrange them,

construct some sort of narrative.

I was looking to find sense in what happened,

fully believing I could.

OUR DOG HAZEL HAS ALWAYS LOVED FOOD TO A PERHAPS INORDINATE DEGREE.

WHEN WE MOVED TO THE MISSION FROM NOE VALLEY, IT DIDN'T TAKE HER LONG TO REALIZE THE STREETS WERE FULL OF POTENTIAL MEALS.

"WHY IS SHE SO EXCITED?"

CHICKEN BONES (FROM POPEYE'S, 23RD & MISSION)

PIZZA CRUSTS

WALKING HER SOON BECAME A STRUGGLE IN WHICH SHE TRIED TO GRAB AND IMMEDIATELY SWALLOW ANYTHING THAT RESEMBLED FOOD

"UH OH"

AND WE TRIED TO STOP HER.

BURRITO, STILL IN FOIL

MUFFIN WRAPPER

MYSTERY TISSUE

HUMAN? ANIMAL?

OH, HOW WE TRIED.

"NO! SPIT IT OUT!"

"DROP IT!"

JMC

EIGHT BLOCKS

JEN OAKS 2010

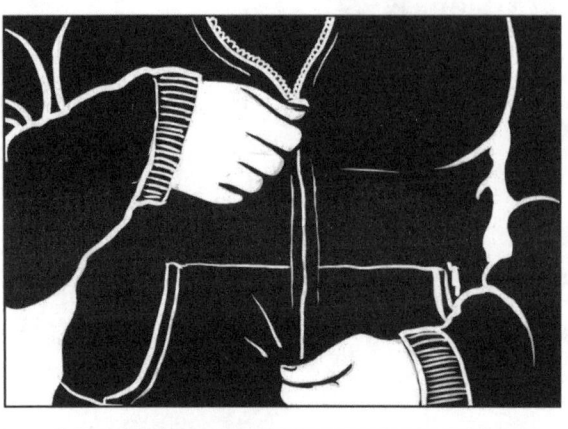

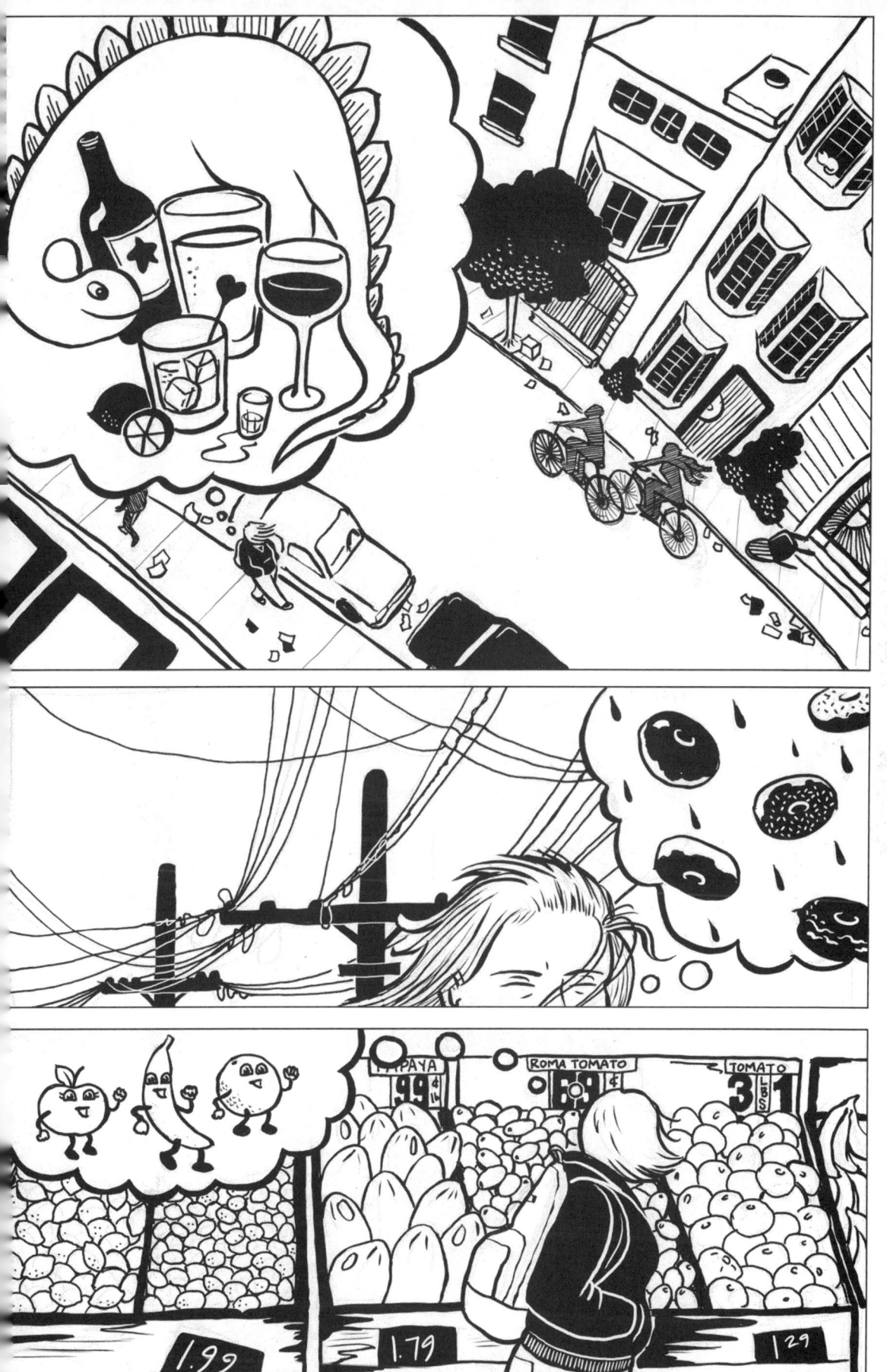

HI! MY NAME IS JEFF — ONE OF MY FAVORITE THINGS TO DO IS TAKE A STROLL DOWN 24TH STREET ON A SUNNY DAY IN THE MISSION!

I LOVE THE SHADY TREES, SMELLS FROM THE BAKERIES AND SEEING FAMILIES OUT TOGETHER — THERE'S SUCH A STRONG SENSE OF COMMUNITY!

BUT SITTING QUIETLY IN THE BACKGROUND IS ONE OF SAN FRANCISCO'S GREATEST ART TREASURES...

THE MURALS OF THE MISSION
By Jeff Walker

AND IF YOU WANT TO SEE MURALS, 24TH ST. IS THE BEST PLACE TO GO! THE STREET ITSELF & THE SURROUNDING AREAS MAY POSSIBLY BE THE DENSEST CONCENTRATION OF MURALS IN THE WORLD!

I MEAN, EVEN THE ELECTRICAL BOXES HAVE MURALS ON THEM!

IS NOTHING SACRED??

BUT WHERE DID THESE MURALS COME FROM? AND WHERE ARE THEY GOING? LET'S TAKE A MOMENT TO SEE HOW THINGS DEVELOPED.

IN THE EARLY '70'S THE STAGE WAS SET. THE MISSION'S PREDOMINANTLY LATINO POPULATION HAD A RICH MURAL TRADITION AND THE NATION WAS REELING FROM THE CIVIL RIGHTS MOVEMENT & VIET NAM WAR PROTEST.

YOUNG ACTIVIST ARTISTS BEGAN EXPRESSING THE CONSCIENCE OF HUMANITY FOR ALL TO SEE. OTHERS WERE DRIVEN TO EDUCATE ON THEIR CULTURAL ROOTS.

EVEN THE LOCAL UNDERGROUND COMIX SCENE GOT IN ON THE ACTION WITH MURALS BY SPAIN RODRIGUEZ AND ROBERT CRUMB.

"CHUNKIN'" BY R. CRUMB (1973)

BUT '74-'75 SAW THE FIRST MAJOR MURAL CLUSTER TAKE SHAPE WITH THE 24TH STREET MINIPARK AT 24TH & YORK FEATURING 8 LARGE SCALE MURALS.

IN 1977 PRECITA EYES MURAL ARTS CENTER WAS FORMED BY MURALIST SUSAN CERVANTES PROMOTING MURAL AWARENESS, OFFERING CLASSES & ORGANIZING COMMUNITY MURAL PROJECTS.

PRECITA EYES 348 STOREFRONT

IN 1984 A GROUP OF 36 ARTISTS CALLED "PLACA" PAINTED 27 MURALS IN BALMY ALLEY OFF 24TH STREET ON THE THEME OF PEACE IN CENTRAL AMERICA. IT HAS SINCE RECEIVED INTERNATIONAL ACCLAIM AND IS MAINTAINED TO THE PRESENT.

PRECITA EYES MURALISTS

THE LATE '80S SAW SEVERAL LARGE SCALE MURALS PAINTED LIKE "SILENT LANGUAGE OF THE SOUL" BY CERVANTES & JUANA ALICIA (22ND & SHOTWELL), "INSPIRE TO ASPIRE" BY MICHAEL RIOS & "LILY ANN" BY CHUY CAMPUSANO:

IN 1992 THE CLARION ALLEY MURAL PROJECT (C.A.M.P.) BEGAN, FILLING ANOTHER ALLEY OF THE MISSION WITH MURALS. THIS TIME THE THEME WAS OF AESTHETIC & DEMOGRAPHIC VARIETY.

THOSE TWENTY YEARS OF ACTIVITY LARGELY DEFINED THE PRESENT LANDSCAPE OF THE MURALS IN THE MISSION. THIS MAP REPRESENTS THEIR PRESENT PROLIFERATION:

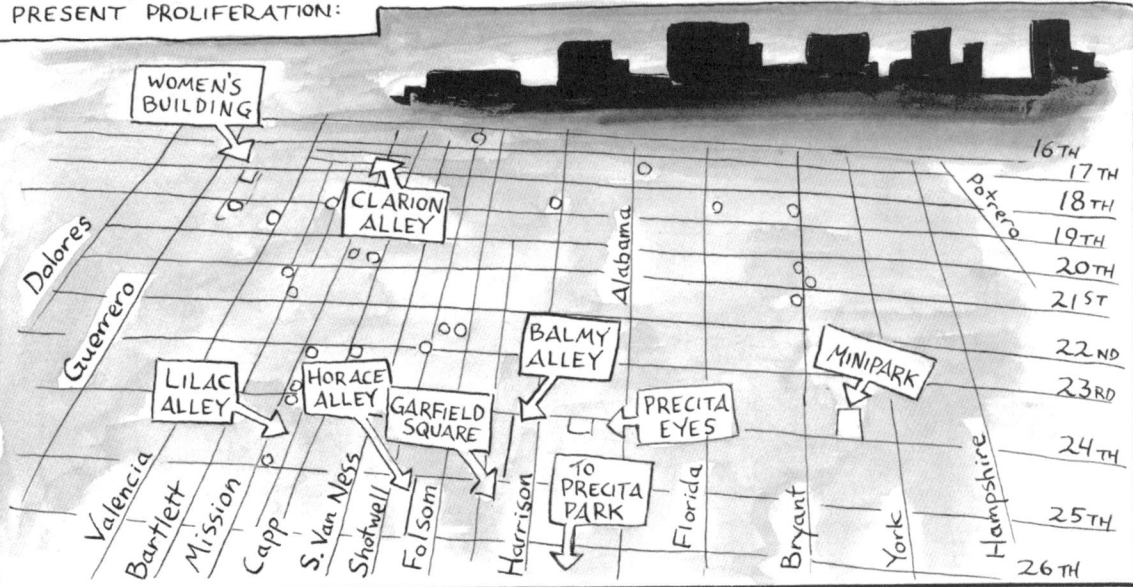

DESPITE SEVERAL AREAS OF CONCENTRATION, THERE ARE STILL PLENTY OF HIDDEN GEMS IN THE NEIGHBORHOOD.

A SIGNIFICANT ASPECT OF ANY MURAL IS HOW IT FITS IN WITH IT'S SURROUNDINGS, SOMETHING ONLY APPRECIATED IN PERSON.

THEREFORE WALKS THROUGH THE NEIGHBORHOOD ARE ALWAYS REWARDING! THERE'S NOTHING LIKE SEEING A STRIKING MURAL FOR THE FIRST TIME. TAKE FOR EXAMPLE...

"MAESTRAPEACE" PAINTED IN 1994 BY JUANA ALICIA, SUSAN CERVANTES, MIRANDA BERGMAN, EDYTH BOONE, MEERA DESAI, YVONNE LITTLETON AND IRENE PEREZ ON THE WOMEN'S BUILDING ON 18TH STREET BETWEEN VALENCIA & GUERRERO WHICH RECOGNIZES SIGNIFICANT WOMEN IN HISTORY AS WELL AS FEMALE FIGURES IN FOLKLORE.

THIS IS NOT THE FIRST MURAL ON THE WOMEN'S BUILDING. PATRICIA RODRIGUEZ PAINTED "WOMEN'S CONTRIBUTION" IN 1982.

RODRIGUEZ, ALONG WITH PEREZ AND CERVANTES WAS ACTIVE IN A GROUP CALLED MUJERES MURALISTAS (WOMEN MURALISTS) WHO HELPED DEFINE THE MURAL LANDSCAPE OF THE MISSION IN THE '70s

THUS AN ADDED SIGNIFICANCE OF MAESTRAPEACE IS IT'S EMBODIMENT OF HOW SUBSTANTIAL WOMEN HAVE BEEN IN THE DEVELOPMENT OF THE MISSION MURAL MOVEMENT.

A PRIME EXAMPLE IS SUSAN CERVANTES, ALREADY MENTIONED AS FOUNDING PRECITA EYES, YET HER PERSONAL CONTRIBUTION OF MURALISM TO THE MISSION STANDS ON IT'S OWN MERIT.

THE STUNNING "FAMILY LIFE" AND "SPIRIT OF MAN" MURALS PAINTED ON LEONARD FLYNN ELEMENTARY SCHOOL CLEARLY DEMONSTRATE THIS. THE MURALS, PAINTED IN '77, FACE PRECITA PARK DIRECTLY ACROSS FROM THE ORIGINAL PRECITA EYES STUDIO.

www.SUSANKCERVANTES.COM
"FAMILY LIFE - SPIRIT OF MAN" ©1977 SUSAN KELK CERVANTES

"THE PRIMAL SEA", COMPLETED IN 1980, IS ONE OF THE EARLIEST MURALS PAINTED BY PRECITA EYES AND CAN STILL BE SEEN AT THE GARFIELD SQUARE POOL LOCATED AT 25TH & HARRISON STREET.

"THE PRIMAL SEA" © 1980 SUSAN KELK CERVANTES

PRECITA EYES EVENTUALLY OPENED A VISITORS CENTER AT 2981 24TH & HARRISON. THEY OFFER MURAL TOURS, FIGURE DRAWING CLASSES & AN ASSORTMENT OF MURAL-RELATED MERCHANDISE.

www.PRECITAEYES.ORG

AND OF COURSE THAT'S JUST DOWN THE STREET FROM BALMY ALLEY.

LET'S DROP IN SHALL WE?

OVER THE YEARS MANY OF THE ORIGINAL MURALS FROM '84 HAVE BEEN REPLACED BUT SOME REMAIN SUCH AS "CULTURE CONTAINS THE SEED OF RESISTANCE WHICH BLOSSOMS INTO THE FLOWER OF LIBERATION" BY MIRANDA BERGMAN & O'BRIEN THIELE.

ONE OF THE NEW ONES, "VICTORION, DEFENDER OF THE MISSION" (2007) BY SIRRON IS ABOUT THE THREAT OF GENTRIFICATION.

THE MURAL USES SIRRON'S SIGNATURE METHOD OF USING CARTOON CUTENESS TO DISARM VIEWERS...

...IN ORDER TO BROACH SERIOUS TOPICS.

SIRRON IS PART OF THE NEW SCHOOL IN MISSION MURALS WHICH UTILIZE POP CULTURE & GRAFITTI STYLE TO RELATE TO THE CURRENT GENERATION.

OTHERS REDEFINE TRADITIONAL FORMS LIKE JOEL BERGNER WHO IS ALMOST A MURALIST REPORTER BECAUSE HE TRAVELS TO OTHER COUNTRIES TO WITNESS THEIR PLIGHT FIRST-HAND BEFORE DEPICTING IT IN A MURAL.

EL INMIGRANTE (2005) 23RD & SHOTWELL

CARTOONISTS REMAIN IN THE MIX WITH CHRIS WARE AND MARK BODE HAVING MURALS ON 826 VALENCIA AND 24TH & LILAC RESPECTIVELY.

OF COURSE I'VE LEFT A LOT OUT PLUS THERE'S PLENTY I DON'T EVEN KNOW ABOUT! BUT HOPEFULLY THIS WHETS YOUR APPETITE!

ALSO I HAVE TO APOLOGIZE PROFUSELY TO ALL THE ARTISTS WHOSE MURALS I HAVE DIMINISHED TO MY MEAGER SCRAWL, BUT IT UNDERSCORES THE POINT: YOU HAVE TO SEE THESE FOR YOURSELF!

AND THANKS TO ALL WHO HELPED.

SO I'LL SEE YOU AROUND THE MISSION, SAN FRANCISCO'S PREMIER ART GALLERY!

HOW IT'S DONE

NOW THAT WE'VE LOOKED AT THE MURAL SCENE IN THE MISSION, YOU MUST SURELY BE WONDERING ABOUT THE PROCESS, SO WE ASKED YUKA, A PRECITA EYES MURAL INSTRUCTOR...

HI!

TODAY WE'RE DOING A MURAL WITH A CLASS FROM JOHN DOE ELEMENTARY SCHOOL:

OK KIDS, WHAT SHOULD THE MURAL BE ABOUT?

BATMAN! DORA! SPONGEBOB!

*NO LICENSED PROPERTIES!

WE NARROW IT DOWN TO 1-3 THEMES.

SO IT WILL BE ABOUT WORLD PEACE AND DINOSAURS.

YAY! COOL!

AS PART OF THE COLLABORATIVE PROCESS, WE HAVE THE KIDS DRAW EACH OTHER'S IDEAS.

BUT I DON'T WANNA DRAW A BUTTERFLY!

THEN WE DO A RECALL EXERCISE TO IDENTIFY THE POIGNANT ELEMENTS.

WHAT DO YOU REMEMBER IS IN OUR MURAL?

A SUN. A STEGOSAURUS. A SNAIL.

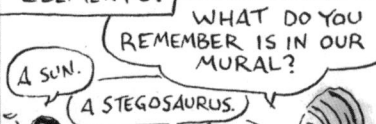

A COMPOSITION IS THEN DESIGNED USING ALL THE FINAL ELEMENTS KEEPING THE DIRECTION OF STORYTELLING IN MIND. SOME POSSIBILITIES ARE:

CENTER OUT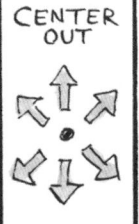

LEFT TO RIGHT / RIGHT TO LEFT

TOP TO BOTTOM

THE FINAL DRAWING IS MADE.

A GRID OF 1" SQUARES IS SUPERIMPOSED OVER THE DRAWING, MAKING SURE TO IDENTIFY THE CENTER AXIS.

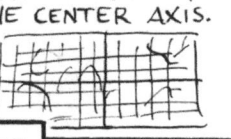

COLOR AND BLACK & WHITE COPIES ARE MADE OF THE DRAWING, THEN WE GO TO THE SITE!

THE FIRST THING TO DO ONSITE IS TO GET THE WALL COMPLETELY CLEAN USING ACETONE BEFORE HOSING IT DOWN.

HEAVE!

THE WALL IS PAINTED WHITE AND A GRID OF 1' SQUARES IS SUPERIMPOSED USING CHALK SNAPLINES TO SCALE UP THE DRAWING. AGAIN THE CENTRAL AXIS IS IDENTIFIED.

THE DRAWING IS TRANSFERRED TO THE WALL IN CHARCOAL AND COATED IN VARNISH SO IT DOESN'T MUDDY THE PAINT.

EVERYONE PUTS ON SOME OLD CLOTHES THEY DON'T MIND GETTING PAINT ON, AND — WE PAINT!! (TOP TO BOTTOM TO AVOID DRIPS)

AFTER PAINTING, WE APPLY SIX COATS OF SPECIAL VARNISH TO PROTECT AGAINST WEATHER, THE SUN & GRAFITTI.

VOILÀ!

Places Seen in the Comics

Eat

Belmar – La Gallinta Meat Market
The Mission Taco
2989 24th St
(between Alabama St & Harrison St)
(415) 826-4600

Bi-Rite Creamery
O Valencia!
3692 18th St
(between Dolores St & Oakwood St)
(415) 626-5600

El Farolito
The Mission Taco
2779 Mission St
(between 23rd St & 24th St)
(415) 824-7877

Four Barrel Coffee
Down on Mission Street
375 Valencia St
(at 15th St)
(415) 252-0800

Luna Park
Sketch
694 Valencia St
(between 18th St & Sycamore St)
(415) 553-8584

St. Francis Fountain
Murray the Attorney
2801 24th St
(between Bryant St & York St)
(415) 826-4200

Beretta
Sketch
1199 Valencia St
(between 22nd St & 23rd St)
(415) 695-1199

Boogaloos
Sketch
3296 22nd St
(between Bartlett St & Valencia St)
(415) 824-4088

Faye's Video & Espresso Bar
Field Notes from the Hipster Habitat
3614 18th St
(between Guerrero St &
Oakwood St)
(415) 522-0434

Katz Bagels & Pizza
All Over Coffee #396
3147 16th St
(between Albion St & Valencia St)
(415) 552-9050

Malai Thai
O Valencia!
3189 16th St
(at Albion St)
(415) 626-8528

Taqueria Cancun
Amity Blamity Presents: The Mission
2288 Mission St
(between 18th St & 19th St)
(415) 252-9560

Taqueria Vallarta
The Mission Taco
3033 24th St
(between Balmy St & Treat Ave)
(415) 826-8116

Ti Couz
O Valencia!
3108 16th St
(at Valencia St)
(415) 252-7373

Weird Fish
Sketch
2193 Mission St
(between Sycamore St & 18th St)
(415) 863-4744

Tartine Bakery
Field Notes from the Hipster Habitat
600 Guerrero St
(between 18th St & 19th St)
(415) 487-2600

El Tonayense
The Mission Taco
3150 24th St.
(between Shotwell St &
Van Ness Ave)
(415) 559-0404

Yo Yo
O Valencia!
3092 16th St
(between Caledonia St & Valencia St)
(415) 255-9181

Drink

Amnesia
Sketch
853 Valencia St
(between 20th St & Cunningham Pl)
(415) 970-0012

Lexington Club
SF Dyke March
3464 19th St
(between Lexington St & Valencia St)
(415) 863-2052

Pop's Bar
Murray the Attorney
2800 24th Street
(between Bryant St & York St)
(415) 401-7677

Delirium
Field Notes from the Hipster Habitat
3139 16th Street
(between Albion St & Valencia St)
(415) 552-5525

Phone Booth
Down on Mission Street
1398 S Van Ness Ave
(between 24th St & 25th St)
(415) 648-4683

Zeitgeist
Murray the Attorney
199 Valencia St
(at Duboce Ave)
(415) 255-7505

Shop

Adobe Bookshop
Sketch
3166 16th Street
(at Albion St)
(415) 864-3936

Community Thrift Store
Buy Used, Buy Bulk
O Valencia!
623 Valencia St
(between 17th St & Clarion Aly)
(415) 861-4910

Mission: Comics and Art
Amity Blamity Presents: The Mission
3520 20th St, Suite B
(between Mission St & San Carlos St)
(415) 695-1545

Paxton Gate
Fragments in the Mission
824 Valencia St
(between 19th St & Cunningham Pl)
(415) 824-1872

Sacred Rose Tattoo
O Valencia!
491 Guerrero St
(between Camp St & 17th St)
(415) 552-5778

Thrift Town
Buy Used, Buy Bulk
2101 Mission St
(between 17th St & Clarion Aly)
(415) 861-1132

Alternative Design Studio –
ADS Hats
No one will ever love me anymore.
418 Valencia St
(between 15th St & Sparrow St)
(415) 503-1316

Goodwill
Buy Used, Buy Bulk
2279 Mission St
(between 18th St & 19th St)
(415) 826-5759

Mission Thrift
Buy Used, Buy Bulk
2330 Mission St
(between 19th St & 20th St)
(415) 821-9560

Rainbow Grocery
Mission Statements
1745 Folsom St
(between 14th St & Erie St)
(415) 863-0621

Therapy
Amity Blamity Presents: The Mission
541 Valencia St
(between 16th St & 17th St)
(415) 865-9758

Visit

Mission Dolores
O Valencia!
3321 16th St
(between Dolores St & Landers St)
(415) 621-8203

Precita Eyes Mural Arts Center
The Murals of the Mission
2981 24th St
(between Alabama St & Harrison St)
(415) 285-2287

SF Armory
O Valencia!
1800 Mission St
(between 14th St & 15th St)
Book Kink.com tours at
SFArmory.com

Spanish-American War Memorial
All Over Coffee #396
Dolores St near Market St

Mission Dolores Park
Fair Weather Friends
Field Notes from the Hipster Habitat
SF Dyke March
18th St to 20th St and
Dolores St to Church St

Roxie Theater
Sketch
3117 16th St
(at Valencia St)
(415) 863-1087

The San Francisco
Women's Building
The Murals of the Mission
3543 18th St
(between Dearborn St & Lapidge St)
(415) 431-1180

Celebrate

Day of the Dead
(Dia de los Muertos)
Mission Statements
November 2nd
dayofthedeadsf.org

San Francisco Carnaval
Mission Statements
End of May
sfcatcarnaval.com

Mexican Independence Day
(El Grito de Dolores)
Mission Statements
September 16th

San Francisco Dyke March
SF Dyke March
Late June
Evening Before the Pride Parade
thedykemarch.org

Contributor Bios

Sean Chiki
dadayama.com

Sean Chiki has enjoyed a lifelong obsession with comics. He is the creator of the comic *Wunderkammer*, as well as being an illustrator, sign painter, musician, and erstwhile theater sound designer. Born in Pittsburgh, he currently lives in San Francisco with his wife and three cats.

Lauren Davis
elledee.com

The mastermind behind this crazy comic book, Lauren Davis spent her first year in San Francisco in an apartment that looked out over the Mission, wondering why it is always so much sunnier and warmer than the rest of the city. When she's not berating cartoonists, Lauren contributes to the popular science fiction blog io9 and writes about webcomics at Storming the Tower.

Jamaica Dyer
jamaicad.com

Jamaica Dyer lives in the Mission, draws comics, and works in animation. Her first graphic novel *Weird Fishes* can be found in comic book stores, and she's currently painting the sequel called *Dee's Siren Song*.

Andrew Farago
williambazillion.com

Andrew Farago is the curator of the Cartoon Art Museum in San Francisco. He has written for Marvel Comics, The Comics Journal, and Animation World Network, and is the author of *The Looney Tunes Treasury*, published by Running Press. His infrequent cartooning work includes the webcomic *The Chronicles of William Bazillion* and occasional mini-comics and projects with his friends in the Bay Area's Couscous Collective. He lives in Berkelely, California with his wife, cartoonist Shaenon K. Garrity.

Shaenon K. Garrity
shaenon.com

Shaenon K. Garrity is the creator of the daily webcomics *Narbonic* and *Skin Horse* (the latter with cowriter Jeffrey C. Wells). She has also written for Marvel Comics and contributed to the anthologies *Broad Appeal*, *Secrets and Lies*, and *I Saw You*. Because none of this makes any money, she works as an editor for manga publisher Viz Media. She and her husband, Andrew Farago, recently moved from the Lower Mission to Berkeley. They miss the cheap sushi.

Justin Hall
allthumbspress.com
Justin Hall is a San Francisco-based cartoonist, who has been producing independent comics since 2001. He won a Xeric Award grant for his first comic book *A Sacred Text*, a fantastical retelling of the story of the Dead Sea Scrolls. After that he began self-publishing his *True Travel Tales* series, which is a collection of autobiographical and biographical stories from the road, featuring everything from anonymous sex in Egyptian temples to blood sacrifices in Bolivia to smuggling cocaine from Peru. Hall's work has also appeared in various other publications, such as the *San Francisco Bay Guardian*, the *Book of Boy Trouble*, *True Porn 2*, *Juicy Mother 2*, *Best Erotic Comics 2008*, *Unsafe For All Ages*, *Stripped*, and more. His character "Glamazonia: The Uncanny Super Tranny" has been hard at work making *Prism Comics: Your LGBT Guide to Comics* more fabulous for several years now. Hall also produces the gay porn comic *Hard To Swallow* with fellow cartoonist Dave Davenport.

Mario Hernandez
One of the infamous Hernandez brothers of *Love and Rockets* fame, Mario Hernandez has been a denizen of the Bay-hey area for over 20 years, contributing to various local comics as well as projects for Fantagraphics and Dark Horse, the latest being *Citizen Rex*.

Greg Hinkle
hinklehaus.blogspot.com
Greg Hinkle has been drawing since he could wrap his little baby fingers around a crayon. After a successful foray into the Northern California fine art scene, including several galleried shows and commissions, he decided to explore further instruction at San Francisco's Academy of Art University. His studies in narrative illustration brought him back to a childhood passion: comic books. He has always been a cartoonist at heart, and tried his hand at comic books starting with self-published mini comics. Greg is currently juggling a growing list of commissioned art and developing several comics projects. He manages to hold it together with an understanding girlfriend and lots and lots of coffee.

Nomi Kane
brewforbreakfast.com
Nomi Kane is a native Berkeleyite, currently working on her MFA at The Center for Cartoon Studies. She's been drawing her autobiographical comic, *Brew for Breakfast*, since 2006. Nomi has self-published several mini-comics, most recently *Chutzpah!* Issue One.

Jonas Madden-Connor
mumblingmynah.com
Jonas Madden-Connor is the creator of the award-winning minicomic *Ochre Ellipse*. He earns money as a graphic designer by day and loses it as a cartoonist by night. He currently lives in Oakland but hopes to one day make the Mission his home again. Naturally, Hazel is very excited about this.

Paul Madonna
paulmadonna.com
Paul Madonna draws and writes the weekly strip *All Over Coffee* for the San Francisco *Chronicle* and SFGate.com, and produces the strip *Small Potatoes* for TheRumpus.net, where he is also comics editor. Paul's work is shown in museums, galleries, restaurants, and cafes, and in 2007 the first collection of *All Over Coffee* was published by City Lights Books, and a forthcoming second collection, *Everything is its own reward*, is due out spring 2011. In 1994 Paul received a BFA from Carnegie Mellon University, and that same year he was the first (ever!) Art Intern at *MAD Magazine*, for which he proudly received no money. Paul currently lives with his wife in San Francisco.

Omar Mamoon
the-mission-taco.blogspot.com
Omar Mamoon was born-and-raised in the SoCal 'burbs of Fullerton, CA. His elder sister first introduced him to "The Mexican Taco" at the mere age of eight when she took him to Taqueria De Anda (taqueriadeanda.com). Here he met the carne asada taco, and it was love at first bite. Omar moved to the Bay Area to pursue a degree in Rhetoric at the University of California, Berkeley. Frustrated with four years of plain, bland hippie tacos, Omar then moved to the Mission District of San Francisco in hopes of finding something a bit more exotic. Overwhelmed with the quality AND quantity of tacos, Omar decided to write a blog on the search for the perfect taco. When he's not eating tacos, Omar is working at an enterprise cloud-computing company. When he's not doing that, he's eating, cooking, and musicing.

Amy Martin
amymartincomics.com
Amy Martin is a cartoonist from Chicago who now lives in San Francisco. She has been self-publishing comic books since 2004, including *The Single Girls* and the *Bachelor Girl* series. Her work deals with women and

the ways we treat each other: friendly and competitive, loving and combative.

John Mathis
mathisink.com

John Mathis has always loved comics and animation. He graduated with a BFA in illustration from the California College of the Arts in 2009 and continues to pursue his dream of working as a professional cartoonist. John currently lives and works in the Bay Area with his girlfriend and two cats (one of which is out to kill him).

Aindrila Mukhopadhyay
flickr.com/photos/aindrila

Aindrila moved to San Francisco in 2002 and is a scientist at the Berkeley Lab. She lives in the Mission with her husband. An enthusiastic weekend artist, her favorite pastime is to wander around the Mission with a sketchpad and camping stool stowed in her backpack. Most of her sketches are ink and pencil, with the occasional use of watercolors. She has spent many happy hours sketching old Mission movie theaters and the dozens of interesting bars and restaurants.

Roman Muradov
bluebed.net

Roman Muradov is an illustrator/writer from cold scary Russia. He loves tea and hates fountains.

Jen Oaks
jenoaks.com

Jen Oaks is an illustrator who used to live at 14th and Guerrero and misses the Mission fiercely. She now lives in Berkeley with her bearded nerd-husband and two cats. Jen is pretty obsessed with vegetables and fancy tea.

Ariel Schrag
arielschrag.com

Ariel Schrag was born in Berkeley, California in 1979. She is the author of the autobiographical graphic novels *Awkward*, *Definition*, *Potential*, and *Likewise*, which chronicle her four years at Berkeley High School. Schrag is currently a writer for the HBO series *How To Make It In America*. She was also a writer for Seasons Three and Four of the hit Showtime series, *The L Word*. Schrag co-writes the online comic *Ariel and Kevin Invade*

Everything with the comedian and writer Kevin Seccia. Schrag's illustrations and comics have appeared in publications such as *The San Francisco Chronicle*, *Time Out New York*, *The Village Voice*, *Juxtapoz*, and *Paper*. Her original art has appeared in museums and galleries across the United States as well as in Austria, Spain, Canada, and the United Kingdom.

Matt Stewart
matt-stewart.com
Matt Stewart lived in the Mission for a surreal, wonderful, occasionally frustrating year. His debut novel, *The French Revolution*, has been called "wildly imaginative," "brilliant," and "an excellent achievement." He's mildly infamous for releasing the novel on Twitter first. Grab his free FrenchRev iPhone app on matt-stewart.com.

Alfred Twu
firstcultural.com
At one point I considered art school, but I'm the kind of person that likes to work collaboratively and remain a bit grounded in reality... so I went to business school instead! Then on orientation day, we had a speaker talk about how companies were hiring people out of art schools because they wanted some creativity. That was back in 2007. Now I'm finishing up my MBA in Sustainable Business at SF State and living in a vegetarian co-op in Berkeley. In addition to comics I also paint murals and manage Bay Area Artists Unite (BAAU), a comic artists' collective in SF, San Jose, and the East Bay. You can contact me at mail@firstcultural.com

Dan V.
danvee.carbonmade.com
danvee.blogspot.com
Born in Los Angeles California, Dan V. writes and draws comic inspired by the Golden Age of Animation. He lives in San Francisco where he spends his days watering his plants and taking long walks with his girlfriend. His favorite movie of all time is *Le Notti De Cabiria* (*Nights of Cabiria*) by Federico Fellini.

Geoff Vasile
geoffvasile.com
Geoff Vasile writes and draws the comic book *Trackrabbit*. He lives in a hellish nightmare world of his own design, and he kind of likes it.

Jeff Walker
jeffsvilleusa.wordpress.com
Jeff Walker, a native of Maryland, graduated from the San Francisco Art Institute in 2004 and subsequently began publishing comics in the *Street Sheet*, a publication of the San Francisco Homeless Coalition, until 2005 when he started the monthly comics newspaper *Madhappys* with some friends, which was published for about a year. In the ensuing years Jeff created several zine-style comics and has painted many cityscapes of San Francisco.

Chuck Whelon
whelon.com
Chuck Whelon is a freelance illustrator and cartoonist based in the Outer Mission. He's produced several series of puzzle and activity books for Dover Publishing, is a regular contributor to *Faces* magazine and has created and illustrated a number of board games for Minion Games. His long running fantasy webcomic serial appears daily at Pewfell.com.

Mike White
amityblamity.blogspot.com
Mike White is from Canada. He now lives in San Francisco. He draws comics while the cats are sleeping. *Amity Blamity Book One* will be available in April 2011 published by SLG Publishing.

Clint Woods
fernetiquette.blogspot.com
Clint Woods has lived in various unfashionable ends of the Mission for a decade or so. Once in a very long while he updates his drinky blog at fernetiquette.blogspot.com. He enjoys long walks on Valencia, devouring grilled cheese and tots at Benders, fog, El Metate, and being less cool than everyone else in the neighborhood.

Rick Worley
rickworley.com
Rick Worley is the creator of *A Waste of Time*, an ongoing series of autobiographical comics in which, for obtuse reasons, he draws himself as a cartoon rabbit. Rick has lived in San Francisco for about two years, which was just long enough for him to fake his way through his entry in this anthology. He divides his time between complaining about his life and lounging around with his legions of sexually submissive twink boy fans. They feed him grapes.

Acknowledgments & Notes

Whew.

When my partner Bill and I first moved to San Francisco, we knew next to nothing about the city, but managed to luck into a South-facing apartment in the Lower Haight. We spent a year looking out over the Mission, and our dog walks, our desire for arts and food – not to mention spectacular people watching – lured us inside. The Mission became our go-to spot for lazy weekends and the first place we'd take out of town guests. We would stuff them with Tartine pastries, tacos, beer, and ice cream until they suspected San Franciscans did nothing besides eat and drink (with occasional pauses to make art).

I love comics because they provide such a wonderful glimpse into other people's brains, and when I decided to collect a comics anthology about a Bay Area neighborhood, the Mission was the logical choice. Selfishly, I wanted to learn more about the Mission, and I was curious to see how it looked through cartoonists' eyes.

The artists and writers of this book did not disappoint. They took me through the past and present of the neighborhood in ways I didn't expect. They accessed their memories and spun some fresh tales. They led me inside places I had only walked by before and gave me a new appreciation for some familiar landmarks. Oh, and they made a lot of cracks about hipsters.

It's been a real pleasure putting this book together, and I hope that you enjoy these comics as much as I have.

I have to thank the many, many people without whom this book would not have been possible (or at least would have been less interesting to read): my partner Bill Heil, who has supported this project from the beginning; Jeff Lester, who offered guidance and much-needed hand holding; all the folks who offered advice, taught me more about the Mission, and put me in touch with so many wonderful cartoonists: James Sime of Isotope Comics, Leef Smith of Mission: Comics and Art (I hope you enjoy your cameo!), Andrew Farago of the Cartoon Art Museum, Shaenon K. Garrity, Matt Silady, and Rio Yañez of the South of Market Cultural Center; and Rachel Dukes of Poseur Ink for answering my frantic late night emails.

Jeff Walker and I both want to thank Precita Eyes for all their help with "The Murals of the Mission" and permission to reproduce their murals.

And, of course, a giant-sized thank you to all of the writers and artists who contributed to this book. Thank you all for your hard work and your patience. I am so honored to publish the work of such a talented group of creators.

A few notes about the individual pieces: "Murray the Attorney," "The Mission Taco," and "Field Notes from the Hipster Habitat" were adapted from longer prose works by Clint Woods, Omar Mamoon, and Matt Stewart respectively. I apologize for cutting so many of their jokes.

"A True Travel Tale" was previously published in Justin Hall's anthology series *True Travel Tales* from All Thumbs Press. "SF Dyke March" was previously published in *How Beautiful the Ordinary: Twelve Stories of Identity* from HarperTeen. "All Over Coffee #396" is from Paul Madonna's series *All Over Coffee*, which appears every Sunday in the San Francisco Chronicle.

The characters in "Amity Blamity Presents: The Mission" are from Mike White's comic series *Amity Blamity*. *Amity Blamity Book One* is coming out from SLG Publishing in May 2011 in finer comic stores everywhere. Check the Preview catalogue in March for ordering info.

That's all she wrote! Happy reading and happy exploring!

-Lauren Davis